I0053016

THE MAGIC OF CHANGE

7 Strategies to Get Unstuck

LYDIA ROY

Foreword by Raymond Aaron

Copyright ©2014 Star Coaching International

All Rights Reserved. No part of this publication may be reproduced, stored in a retrieval system, or transmitted, in any form or by any means, electronic, mechanical, photocopying, recording, or otherwise, without the prior written permission of the author, Lydia Roy. Printed in Canada.

AUTHOR	Lydia Roy
SUBSTANTIVE EDITOR	Liz Culotti
DESIGN AND LAYOUT	Liz Culotti
CONTRIBUTING ARTIST	Brienne Juniper
COVER ARTIST	Pixel Studios

Published by the Raymond Aaron Group

THE RAYMOND AARON GROUP™
1-9225 LESLIE ST.
RICHMOND HILL
ONTARIO, CANADA
L4B 3H6

WWW.AARON.COM

FOREWORD BY RAYMOND AARON

The Magic of Change: 7 Strategies to Get Unstuck by Lydia Roy will help you understand that you can achieve any goal you set for yourself, as long as you are willing to commit to making a change in your life. Change is not easy; it can take time, however at the end of it, if you have a plan and strategy, you can and will be successful. How you succeed is how you change. This book will encourage you to challenge yourself, find your strengths and values, and learn to trust your process of change. Lydia's unique ability to ask deep, meaningful questions will help you, step-by-step, through your change process. By being truthful to yourself about what you really want out of life, you will find huge success through this book.

TABLE OF CONTENTS

INTRODUCTION

"Everyone thinks of changing the world, but no one thinks of changing himself."
- Leo Tolstoy

If I asked most of you if you are living to your full potential, what would you say? What if I asked you if you were satisfied with your current reality, or if you have achieved all of your goals?

We all set goals to inspire ourselves to achieve a new level in our careers, our relationships, or our lives in general. We want to experience ourselves contributing something, so we set expectations for ourselves that require us to change what we do and how we do it in order to make that difference. Making a change is fundamentally about movement. Movement from where you are today to where you want to go. But it is not always easy and it is not always a conscious choice we make.

There is a process to change, and by working through the following seven chapters, you will discover that process and how it works for you. This book is a blueprint that can help you move from where you are towards the goal that you are really wanting, in any area of life. It is a step-by-step system, and the book itself allows you to practice this system with any goal you currently want to achieve.

This book will help you through your change with tips, quizzes, step-by-step processes, and questions that will force you to take a closer look at how you operate. It will ask you to identify your fears, what has been holding you back from making the change you want to make, and lead you down a path that will break through those fears and bring you closer to your goal.

Write your answers directly in this book; think of it as your Change Workbook. Answer the questions honestly, as this is for your eyes only. At the end of every chapter you will find a Learning Cycle, as well as Five Reflective Questions that will help you to summarize your learnings from the previous chapter.

Give yourself time to work through each chapter; take a week if you need it. Revisit the chapter and do the exercises as many times as you want to until you are ready to move to the next step.

What Do I Want?
MAKING A CHANGE

How Do I Trust
My Way of Making
A Change?
**TRUSTING
YOUR PROCESS**

Where Am I Now?
**SEEING IS
BELIEVING**

SEVEN
STRATEGIES
TO GET
UNSTUCK

What Will Make
A Change Last?
**INSPIRIED
MENTORSHIP**

What Is The
Best I Have?
**DIRECTION
OF STRENGTH**

How Do I Learn
From Change?
**INSPIRING
THE SPIRIT**

What Can Get
In The Way?
KEEPING ON

MAKING A CHANGE

"Once you make a decision, the universe conspires to
make it happen."
-Ralph Waldo Emerson

WHAT DO I WANT?

Whether you have a clear intention to make a change or are being
forced into change, you must have a clear, conscious focus on your
end goal in order to successfully make this change in your life.

Ask yourself the following questions to become even clearer on
your goal:

What do I really want?

_____

_____

What is important about this change for me?

_____

_____

What will it mean if I do not make the change?

_____

_____

What is a picture or image that best describes the change I want?

_____

_____

How will I know when I have made the change?

_____

_____

What are three tangible measures of success that I will experience when I make the change?

a. _____

_____

b. _____

_____

c. _____

_____

FEAR VS. POSSIBILITY

Change can happen for a number of reasons. Maybe you are feeling unhappy, maybe you have a specific desire for improvement, or maybe something has happened that is forcing a change.

Whether the change is forced upon you or whether you have chosen it yourself, it is natural to experience a sense that you are losing something. You are. You are losing the familiar. You may experience uncertainty, confusion, and loss. Change at its core requires letting go: letting go of the familiar, the known, and the comfortable and moving from your comfort zone to a place that can stretch you out of your comfort zone. So what is getting in your way?

> "Fear is like an anchor holding us back;
> sometimes we have to let go of who we are to
> become what we could be."
> - Anonymous

The letting go phase is the beginning of change. If you are serious about making a change, understand that what you have always done before is not going to support you. So now is the time to take steps you have never taken.

In the chart below, make a list of feelings of fear and feelings of possibility related to making change.

FEELINGS OF FEAR	FEELINGS OF POSSIBILITY
What are you giving up by making the change?	What would you receive as a result of making the change?
What are you most afraid of?	What is there to learn about yourself?
What happens if you do the same things you have always done?	What is possible for you once you have made the change?
•	•
•	•
•	•
•	•
•	•
•	•
•	•
•	•
•	•

For tips on how to diminish your voice of Inner Judgment so you can feel the fear and do it anyway, go to my website, www.lydiaroy.com.

THREE STEPS TO A SUCCESS MINDSET

Your goal will take a life of its own if you have prepared yourself for it.

STEP 1: Write Down Your Goal.

People who are successful in achieving their goals are personally committed to it. They have important reasons for achieving their goal and can speak of it in a sentence that will tell you specifically what they are going to do. For example, "I am going to lose 10 lbs. in the next 30 days so that I am healthier and have more energy." It is also important to have a clear, tangible way of knowing that your goal has been achieved.

Ask yourself the following questions:

What is my goal?

_____

_____

Why is it important to me?

_____

_____

What will it mean if I do not achieve this goal?

_____

_____

How realistic is my goal?

_____

_____

By when would I like it to be achieved?

_____

_____

How will I know I have been successful?

_____

_____

What would be an even better result?

_____

_____

STEP 2: Feeling the Success

You have to be internally ready to move forward by having trust and positive expectation that the goal you are moving towards is going to happen. Enjoy the process of change by keeping the feeling of your eventual success inside you.

Know that it is the feeling of believing that is going to make change happen. When you can create within yourself a good feeling about the results you want, you connect into what is truly at the centre and in alignment for you. You begin to believe that this change has already happened. You live as if it is already done. The result is there. There is no difference between this new step you are taking and reality: it already exists.

The first step is to be clear about your goal. In order to bring your future forward, become extremely clear on what that desired future actually is. Close your eyes and imagine that you are inside your goal and that it has already been accomplished.

What do I see for myself?

_____

_____

How does it feel?

_____

_____

Align with Your Goal
- Imagine it through your five senses. What do you see, feel, taste, hear, and smell?
- Ask your gut or intuition to offer its perspective to you.
- Imagine a bridge between that good feeling and your future goal.
- Breathe in the goal and visualize it again
- Imagine and draw into you all those people and resources that can help you make your goal a reality.

Do this exercise as often as you can throughout the day. Be with it for about two or three minutes, and then let it go. The essence of this exercise is to figure out the result you want, bring it forward, and connect it with your senses and the feeling that it gives you when you have achieved the result.

STEP 3: Affirmations

Affirmations are clear statements of what you want, why it is important to you, and why you would be grateful to receive it. Regular and positive affirmations are key to shifting your mindset.

Keep repeating your affirmations over and over again, morning and evening. Think of the positive thoughts that are going to support you in achieving your goal. Every morning, be grateful for what is already there and affirm what is working. Every evening, be thankful for what has happened that day and what you have accomplished.

MORNING EXERCISE

"I am grateful for...."

1. _____

2. _____

3. _____

4. _____

5. _____

6. _____

7. _____

8. _____

9. _____

10. _____

EVENING EXERCISE

"I'm grateful for this today..."

1. _____

2. _____

3. _____

4. _____

5. _____

6. _____

7. _____

8. _____

9. _____

10. _____

FIVE QUESTIONS FOR REFLECTION:
MAKING A CHANGE

1. WHAT HAS INSPIRED YOU TO MAKE THIS CHANGE?

_____

_____

_____

_____

2. HOW DID YOU PREPARE YOURSELF FOR THIS CHANGE?

_____

_____

_____

_____

3. WHAT MEANING WILL THIS CHANGE HAVE FOR YOU?

_____

_____

_____

_____

4. WHAT IS THE MOST IMPORTANT MEASURE OF SUCCESS FOR
    YOU WHILE ACHIEVING YOUR CHANGE?

_____

_____

_____

_____

5. WHAT REWARD WOULD BE MEANINGFUL TO YOU AS YOU
    CONTINUE TO TAKE STEPS TOWARDS YOUR GOAL?

_____

_____

_____

_____

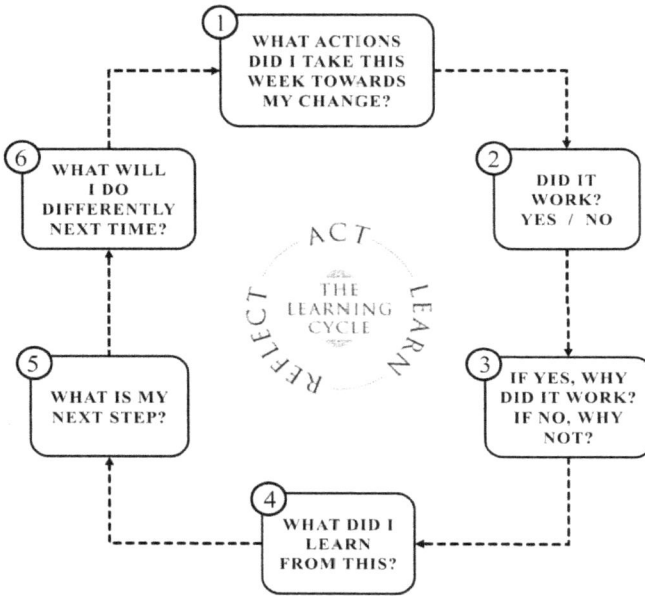

1 WHAT ACTIONS DID I TAKE THIS WEEK TOWARDS MY CHANGE?

6 WHAT WILL I DO DIFFERENTLY NEXT TIME?

2 DID IT WORK? YES / NO

ACT
THE LEARNING CYCLE
REFLECT
LEARN

5 WHAT IS MY NEXT STEP?

3 IF YES, WHY DID IT WORK? IF NO, WHY NOT?

4 WHAT DID I LEARN FROM THIS?

1. _____
2. _____
3. _____
4. _____
5. _____
6. _____

SEEING IS BELIEVING

"You must understand that seeing is believing,
but also know that believing is seeing."
- Denis Waitley

WHERE AM I NOW?

Your current reality is a statement that, if you look at it factually, realistically and honestly, will tell you what you believe in and what you are currently accepting in your life. To better understand what you believe in, just look around you. What you believe is what you see and what you see is what you believe. Your life, what you are doing, the activities you are involved in, the results that are coming forward, all the things that are tangible around you will reflect your beliefs back to you.

Once you have decided to make a change, it is important to be aware of your current reality and compare it to your desired reality. This will create tension between the two realities and pull you towards what you really want. Look at your life and say, "This is where I am, and that is where I want to be." Get clear on the reasons for the change you want to make.

THE BELIEF WHEEL

The eight sections of the Belief Wheel on page 17 represent the eight most important areas of your life. Whatever currently exists in your life is connected to your current belief system. If you can take an honest look and pinpoint what you are happy or unhappy with and why, you will get a clear understanding of what you believe in.

For example, let's say you rank your environment at 3 out of 10. What makes it a 3? What beliefs do you have that are informing the way you are ranking your satisfaction with what you currently have in your life? Maybe you have a belief around being environmentally friendly, but you drive an SUV. In this case, your environment is not aligning with your beliefs.

Rank your level of satisfaction with each of these 8 areas of your life.

THE BELIEF WHEEL

RANK YOUR SATISFACTION FROM 0 - 10

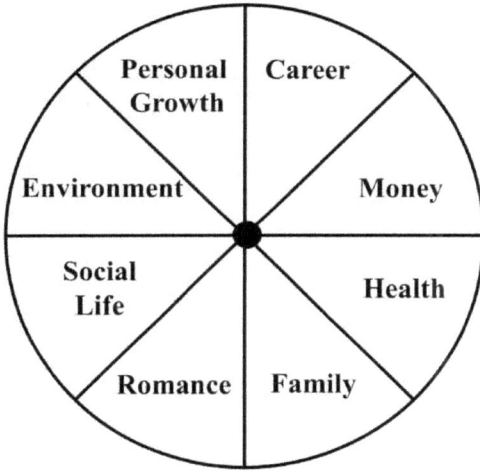

Personal Growth | Career | Money | Health | Family | Romance | Social Life | Environment

CAREER _____

MONEY _____

HEALTH _____

FAMILY _____

ROMANCE _____

SOCIAL LIFE _____

PERSONAL GROWTH _____

ENVIRONMENT _____

In which area am I most satisfied?

_____
_____
_____

What makes the satisfaction level so high in this area of my life?

_____
_____
_____

In which area am I least satisfied?

_____
_____
_____

What makes the satisfaction level so low in this area of my life?

_____

_____

What will it take to bring my level of satisfaction up in the area I am interested in changing?

_____

_____

What, if anything, is stopping me from making these changes?

_____

_____

With all the changes happening in the world today, we are meant to be in connection with ourselves and in full abundance in all areas of our lives. This begins by looking on the inside first. There are many tools that help us do a check in on ourselves. To download your Personal Abundance Guide, please go to my website, www.lydiaroy.com.

FIVE QUESTIONS FOR REFLECTION:
SEEING IS BELIEVING

1. WHAT DID YOU LEARN ABOUT YOUR CURRENT SITUATION OR ISSUE?

_____

_____

_____

_____

2. WHERE IS THE BIGGEST GAP BETWEEN YOUR CURRENT REALITY AND YOUR DESIRED FUTURE?

_____

_____

_____

_____

3. WHAT BEHAVIOURS MAY BE REQUIRED TO MOVE FROM YOUR CURRENT SELF TO YOUR FUTURE SELF?

_____

_____

_____

_____

4. WHAT IN YOUR CURRENT REALITY ALIGNS WITH YOUR DESIRED CHANGE?

_____

_____

_____

_____

5. ON A SCALE OF 1-10, HOW COMMITTED ARE YOU TO MOVING TOWARDS YOUR DESIRED CHANGE AND FUTURE SELF?

_____

_____

_____

_____

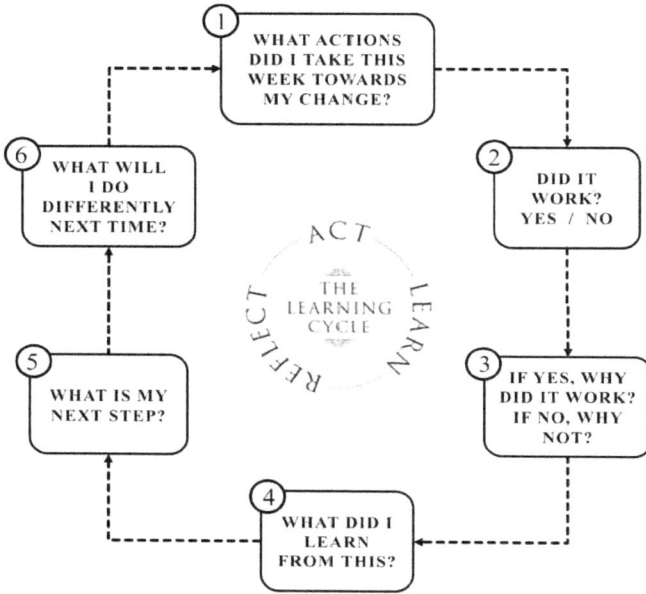

1. _____

2. _____

3. _____

4. _____

5. _____

6. _____

THE DIRECTION OF STRENGTH

"Understand that the right to choose your own path is a sacred privilege. Use it. Dwell in possibility."
- Oprah Winfrey

WHAT IS THE BEST I HAVE TO WORK WITH?

There is not one best way to achieve your goal; there are just different ways, all equally effective depending on who you are as a person. When you make a change, it is important to decide how you are going to implement this change. What are your strengths? How can they best support you as you work towards your goal?

Tune into your thoughts and be aware of whether they are coming from a place of strength or weakness. It is hard to connect with your strengths if you are coming from a place of fear or doubt. In the mindset of weakness, we look at what is wrong or who is to blame and try to keep the status quo. But from the mindset of strength, we look at what is working, what is possible, and what we can learn.

It is easy to forget who we are and what we are good at, especially in times of stress. Your own past is a clue to your strengths and gifts. What has helped you to succeed in the past? What works for you? These are the things that will be useful to focus on, particularly when you are struggling.

Focusing on strengths helps you to manifest your change or your goal faster because you are focusing in on what you do best. This gives you confidence and eliminates obstacles that can get in your way. For a Strengths Checklist, go to my website, www.lydiaroy.com. This tool will help you to create a compelling strengths list that will remind you of who you are at your best.

BE AWARE OF HOW YOU FEEL

How can you shift your mindset to the place of strength and possibility? How do you, at these times of stress or struggle, bring yourself to the person you know you really are? The beginning is having an awareness of what state you are in. Then, have awareness around how you have moved through the state of stress to operate from your strengths. Most important are the emotions you experience when you are operating from your strengths or when you are operating from your weaknesses.

What are three adjectives that describe my feelings when I am operating from my strengths?

a. _____

_____

b. _____

_____

c. _____

_____

What are three adjectives that describe my feelings when I am not operating from my strengths?

a. _____

_____

b. _____

_____

c. _____

_____

LISTEN TO YOUR STORIES

When have you accomplished something that you were really proud of, either in your personal or professional life. For example, running a marathon for a great cause or succeeding at something challenging that made you step outside of your comfort zone.

Tell your story:

_____

_____

_____

_____

_____

_____

_____

What are two other similar experiences you have had? Tell the stories below.

a. _____

_____

b. _____

_____

What are two similarities you see between these stories?

a. _____

_____

b. _____

_____

"When I am most fulfilled, I am..."
(e.g. connected with others, exploring something new, free to contribute in my own way)

_____

_____

START SMALL

Start making small steps towards your desired reality. Beginning to change can be very overwhelming, but starting small, creating a plan, using the resources around you, and even asking for help are all ways for you to get started.

In the table on the next page write a list of tasks to complete in order to get to your goal. After each task, write a list of pros and cons. Then, write three summary statements that will help you to keep going.

TASK	PROS	CONS
Go to the gym	• be healthy • • • • • •	• have to find the time • • • • • •

SUMMARY STATEMENTS

e.g. finding a convenient time to go to the gym to ensure consistency

1.
2.
3.

APPLY HABITS FOR SUCCESS

What good habits do you have that will support your strengths? What bad habits do you have that do not support your strengths? Replace them with habits that do support your strengths, for example watching too much TV instead of doing something productive with your time that can support your overall goal.

Decide which habits or activities to stop, to start, and what to keep doing.

STOP DOING: COMPLETE:

1. _____   ☐

2. _____   ☐

3. _____   ☐

KEEP DOING:

1. _____   ☐

2. _____   ☐

3. _____   ☐

START DOING:

1. _____   ☐

2. _____   ☐

3. _____   ☐

GET RESOURCEFUL

There may be useful resources, whether articles, books or people, which can provide you with knowledge around your goal, or something similar. Read what is available or interview whomever you can and write down bullet points around what you need to pay attention to. This will give you a step-by-step structure for you to follow. Pay attention to the top 5 "How To's" of how a goal similar to yours has been achieved.

RESOURCE	HOW TO'S
1.	›
	›
	›
	›
2.	›
	›
	›
	›
3.	›
	›
	›
	›
	›

FIVE QUESTIONS FOR REFLECTION:
THE DIRECTION OF STRENGTH

1. DID YOU LIVE UP TO YOUR EXPECTATIONS TODAY?

    _____
    _____
    _____
    _____

2. WHAT WAS THE RESULT OF PAYING ATTENTION TO WHO YOU
    ARE AT YOUR BEST?

    _____
    _____
    _____
    _____

3. WHAT WAS DIFFICULT ABOUT IT AND WHAT DID YOU LEARN?

    _____
    _____
    _____
    _____

4. WHAT ADVICE WOULD YOU GIVE TO OTHERS AROUND
    LIVING THEIR BEST SELF?

    _____
    _____
    _____
    _____

5. WHAT IS A MANTRA OR SAYING YOU CAN GIVE TO YOURSELF
    TO REMIND YOU OF THE BEST SELF THAT YOU ARE?

    _____
    _____
    _____
    _____

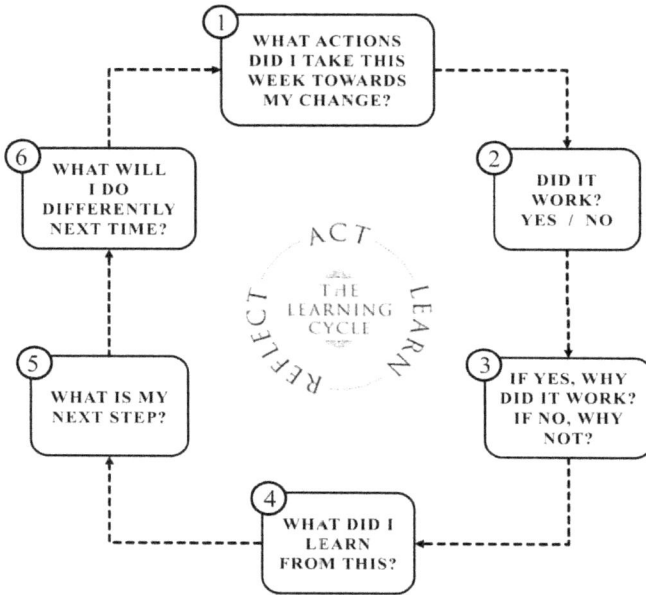

1. _____

2. _____

3. _____

4. _____

5. _____

6. _____

Keeping On

"We are made to persist. That's how we find out who
we are."
- Tobias Wolff

What Can Get in the Way?

Once we decide to make a change in our lives, it is not easy to
stick to it and stay motivated. It is easy to lose focus and become
complacent, especially when the change is big and takes longer
than you were initially expecting.

Come to terms with uncertainty. Each step you take will bring you
closer to where you are supposed to be, even if that is difficult to
believe in the present moment.

Beware of having firm expectations of how your goal is going to
be realized. Expect that obstacles are going to get in your way and
potentially stop you from realizing your goal. Be open to the
possibility that you will reach your goal, even if it happens in the
most unexpected way. Be confident in the fact that it will happen
if you stay the course.

Sometimes the best thing you can do
is the next thing really well.

If you find that you can no longer see a concrete end goal, just do what is best with what is right in front of you. Andy Murray, winner of Wimbledon 2013, has practiced his serve thousands of times so that *every single time* he serves at his best. The lesson here is to put your all into every step you take because it *will* lead you to your goal, even if you cannot see it.

REMEMBER YOUR PURPOSE

It is also helpful to go back to the beginning and remember *why* you wanted to make a change in the first place. Maybe you were unhappy in your career or one of your relationships, or maybe you wanted to become more successful in a certain aspect of your life. Whatever your reason for change, remind yourself of it as often as you can.

What will it mean to me if I make the change?

_____

_____

What will it mean to me if I do not make the change?

_____

_____

How will this change align with what I most believe in and value?

_____

_____

OVERCOMING OBSTACLES

When you feel stuck and unable to move forward with your goal, the best thing you can do is assess and draw from the resources and support available to you. Look around you, identify them, and use them to your advantage.

QUESTIONNAIRE

On a scale of 1 to 5, 1 being completely ready for change and 5 not at all, where am I in terms of my change readiness continuum?

Very Ready	Mostly Ready	Ready	Unsure	Scared
1	2	3	4	5

When I am faced with an obstacle, how often am I able to overcome it?

Very Often	Often	Sometimes	Rarely	Never
1	2	3	4	5

How many external barriers are keeping me from my goal? Add up the number of obstacles that are getting in the way.

- □ Time
- □ Lack of support
- □ Lack of relationships (networking)

- □ Money
- □ Lack of knowledge
- Total:_____

How many internal barriers are keeping me from my goal? Add up the number of obstacles that are getting in the way.

- □ Habits
- □ Beliefs & values
- □ Lack of personal commitment & focus

- □ Inner critic
- □ Fear of giving up too much
- Total:_____

When change feels awkward or I feel ill at ease, what level of support do I currently have?

Very High	High	Average	Low	Very Low
1	2	3	4	5

How often am I able to stay positive when I am confronted with obstacles?

Very Often	Often	Sometimes	Rarely	Never
1	2	3	4	5

On a scale of 1-5, how aware am I of strategies that will keep me motivated when I want to give up?

Very Aware	Mostly	Aware	Somewhat	Not Aware
1	2	3	4	5

How often do I reach out to others for support?

Very Often	Often	Sometimes	Rarely	Never
1	2	3	4	5

On a scale of 1-5, how often does the worry of giving up a personal need hold me back from making a change? For example, losing money or starting over somewhere new.

Never	Rarely	Sometimes	Often	Very Often
1	2	3	4	5

How often and how easily am I able to acknowledge my successes?

Very Often	Often	Sometimes	Rarely	Never
1	2	3	4	5

MY SCORE:

/50

RESULTS

SCORE 1-12 - VERY GOOD! You're on the right track, but you're also here for a reason. Stick with what has worked for you in the past, but make sure there is nothing holding you back from becoming the best YOU you can be!

SCORE 13-25 - GOOD! There are a few things holding you back, but you should be able to acknowledge them and work through them pretty easily now that you're aware of them. If you need help making some small changes, don't hesitate to ask for it. It can be hard to make such a big change on your own.

SCORE 26-38 - ROAD WORK AHEAD! You have a lot of work to do, but don't lose heart, because it can be done! Take a good look at everything that is holding you back and ask yourself why you have created so many obstacles for yourself. If your passion and motivation for change is strong enough, you should be able to overcome anything with some help from your support system.

SCORE 39-50 - UH OH! Seems like everything gets in your way and stops you from accomplishing what you think you want. Take a closer look at your goal and make sure it's what you REALLY want. If it truly aligns with all of your values and strengths, make sure you reach out to your support system and ask for help. You are definitely your own worst enemy and you need to make some changes before you will be able to accomplish what you want to in life.

THE GROAN ZONE

If you have taken the questionnaire and your score is high, you might be in what I like to call "The Groan Zone." Your anxiety around change is diluting your motivation, you are feeling overloaded, your priorities are confused, and you are filled with feelings of uncertainty and frustration. This is normal!

Resistance to change is natural because we, as humans, have a fundamental need for certainty. We are always searching for our "normal" place, so we seek to get back to a routine. Usually when we resist change it is because of fear of being outside of our "normal" state. Even if our current conditions are not good and change is needed, people still prefer the things that they know.

When you are in "The Groan Zone," you need a support network, whatever that may be for you. For example, set routine work hours for yourself, or find a coach who will hold you accountable. Create a temporary process to help you through this tough time. Sometimes the goal is so big you have to set smaller, more definable goals that are easy to manage and can build your confidence. Stay in the present moment versus focusing on how far you are away from your goal. Focus on what is working for you in the moment. The main goal here is to find something that will give you defined time frames within which to accomplish your goal, step by step.

On the next page you will find some common thoughts or excuses we tell ourselves when we are deep in "The Groan Zone," and some things to think about or actions to take in order to counter the "language of resistance" we have created in our own minds.

RECOGNIZING THE "LANGUAGE OF RESISTANCE"

EXCUSE	COUNTER THOUGHT
"There are no guarantees that this will work."	Understand that change is about loss and the unknown.
"I am fine just the way I am."	What will it mean if you don`t make this change today?
"There will be unanticipated curves in the road."	Create a step by step process to define steps more clearly. The support of a mentor with similar experience may be helpful.
"I'm too busy to think about this right now"	There will always be things that can get in your way if you let them. If this change is a priority, make it one.

FIVE QUESTIONS FOR REFLECTION:
KEEPING ON

1. CAN YOU THINK OF A TIME WHEN YOU THOUGHT YOU WOULD NEVER ACHIEVE YOUR GOAL? WHAT DID YOU DO AND HOW DID YOU OVERCOME IT?

_____

_____

_____

_____

2. WHAT HELPS YOU MANAGE YOUR OWN LANGUAGE OF RESISTANCE?

_____

_____

_____

_____

3. HOW CAN YOU MINIMIZE THE UNKNOWN AND FOCUS YOUR EFFORTS ON ACHIEVING YOUR CHANGE OR GOAL?

_____

_____

_____

_____

4. WHAT IS THE BEST WAY TO CAPTURE AND USE WHAT WORKS FOR YOU TO MAKE THE CHANGE THAT YOU WANT?

_____

_____

_____

_____

5. HOW CAN YOU MANAGE YOUR TIME EFFECTIVELY SO THAT YOU BECOME PROACTIVE AND NOT REACTIVE?

_____

_____

_____

_____

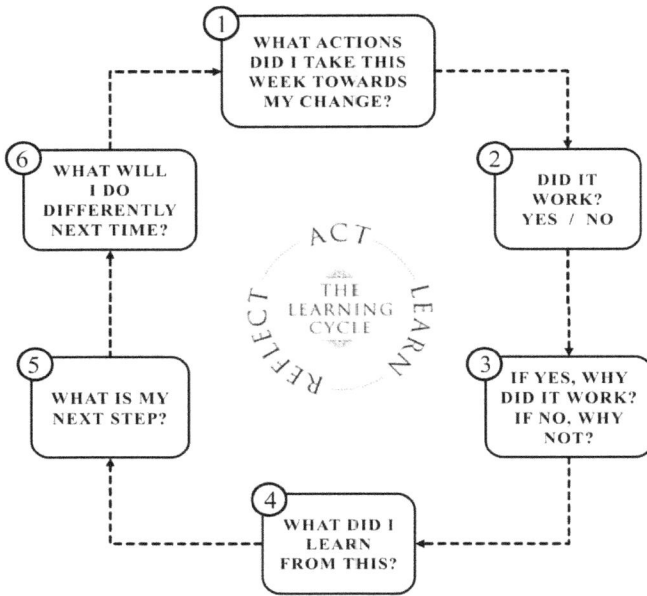

1. _____

2. _____

3. _____

4. _____

5. _____

6. _____

INSPIRING THE SPIRIT

"Always dream and shoot higher than you know you
can do. Don't bother just to be better than your
contemporaries or predecessors. Try to be better than
yourself."
- William Faulkner

HOW DO I LEARN FROM CHANGE?

How do you learn from the change you are going through? The
change process is about learning what works and what does not
work and then adjusting your actions to make sure they will bring
you to your end goal.

Treat this as a time of learning and be open to a whole new self-
discovery of who you might be when the unfolding is uncertain.
Let the fuzziness and unpredictability be a teacher that inspires
you to ask what it wants from you at this time and who you need
to be to help yourself through this change. Change can come
slowly and you may go through many ups and downs, but instead
of being discouraged, take learning from them and use that learning
to keep moving forward. Take the time to fix whatever the problem
is and make sure that it does not happen again.

"What can you do to strengthen your spirit? 'It can be as simple as vowing to ourselves that we absolutely refuse to surrender our spirit to circumstances.'"
- Price Pritchett, The Unfolding

This kind of reflection requires a mindset of telling the truth to yourself, of being present, and of being completely available, mind, heart, and spirit, to what is occurring.

ACKNOWLEDGE & ADJUST

Acknowledge what you have done successfully and pay close attention to the things that are a challenge or that need adjustment.

What are three things I have accomplished so far?

a. _____

_____

b. _____

_____

c. _____

_____

What are three actions that have taken me backwards?

a. _____

_____

b. _____

_____

c. _____

_____

What are three actions or behaviours that will move me forward towards my goal?

a. _____

_____

b. _____

_____

c. _____

_____

STAY IN THE MOMENT

Stay focused in the moment so that you can experience what you are thinking about and find a way to keep your thoughts optimistic and appreciative, no matter how many setbacks you have encountered.

What am I most hoping for and dreaming about as it relates to my change?

_____

_____

What will it mean to me when I get there?

_____

_____

What are some of the positive emotions I will feel when I have achieved my goal (Highlight any that apply)?

OPEN   HOPEFUL
HAPPY   STRONG
ALIVE   ENCOURAGED
LOVE   CONFIDENT
INTERESTED

What are some of the negative emotions I will feel if I do not achieve my goal?

ANGRY   AFRAID
DEPRESSED   HURT
CONFUSED   SAD
HELPLESS   DISILLUSIONED
INDIFFERENT   INCAPABLE

FIVE QUESTIONS FOR REFLECTION:
INSPIRING THE SPIRIT

1. WHAT ONE CHANGE DID YOU NEED TO MAKE THIS WEEK TO CONTINUE YOUR PROCESS?

_____

_____

_____

_____

2. WHAT ONE DISCOVERY DID YOU MAKE ABOUT WHAT CHALLENGES YOU IN THIS CHANGE PROCESS?

_____

_____

_____

_____

3. WHAT STRENGTHS HAVE SERVED YOU WELL AS YOU GO THROUGH YOUR CHANGE PROCESS?

_____

_____

_____

_____

4. WHAT CONTINUES TO WORK WELL TOWARDS THE RESULT THAT YOU ARE SEEKING?

_____

_____

_____

_____

5. WHAT IS ONE WORD TO DESCRIBE YOUR MINDSET DURING THIS CHANGE PROCESS?

_____

_____

_____

_____

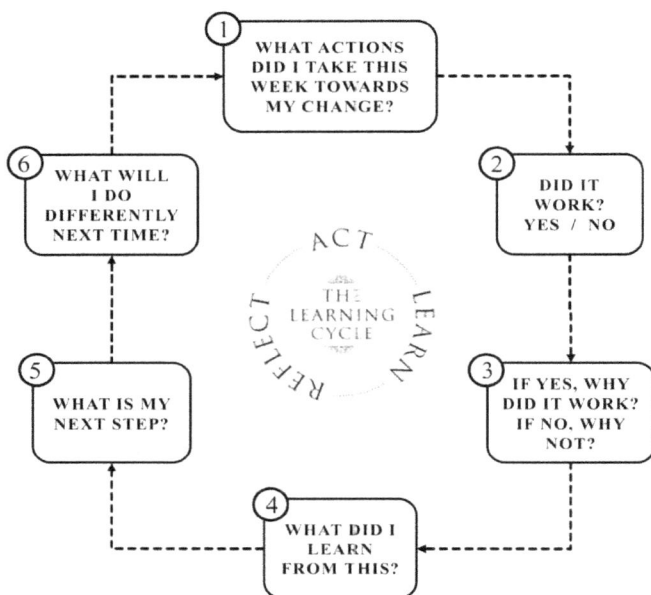

1. _____
2. _____
3. _____
4. _____
5. _____
6. _____

INSPIRED MENTORSHIP

"I've learned that people will forget what you said,
people will forget what you did, but people will never
forget how you made them feel."
— Maya Angelou

WHAT WILL MAKE CHANGE LAST?

Throughout this change process, you have hopefully become more
aware of your behaviours and practices and realized that in order
to succeed, you have to do things differently than you did before.
You have encountered setbacks, been stuck, overcome obstacles,
lost focus, and found yourself. The change has happened and you
are on your way to reaching your goal, so how do you make sure
this change lasts?

Find a mentor who believes in you; someone who has the
experience you need and who will support you, build your self-
confidence, and help you acknowledge all that you have
accomplished along the way. When you accept that you cannot do

this alone, you will find someone to go on this journey with you, sharing in your ups and downs and investing in your outcome.

INSPIRED MENTORSHIP

What is mentorship? Do not just think that a successful friend you admire will be the perfect mentor for you, or that hiring the first coach someone recommends to you will solve all your problems. Look for someone who has already accomplished what you want for yourself. Make sure their speciality aligns with your goals. An inspired mentor is someone who is invested in you, your business, and the change you are making. They will collaborate with you, share thoughts and suggestions, help you identify your next steps, and focus on what you need to reach your goal.

Your mentor should know your strengths, weaknesses, values, and motivators, and be responsive to whatever is important in the moment. This is a partnership that will maintain motivation, make change last, and keep you on track to your end goal without falling back into the same old habits.

DEFINING YOUR EXPECTATIONS

What are three things that I hope to gain from a partnership with an inspired mentor. (e.g. I will learn new things, I will have the support I need to reach my goal)

a. _____

_____

b. _____

_____

c. _____

_____

Has someone ever inspired me to make a change in my life? If yes, who, and how did they inspire me to make that change?

_____

_____

What are three characteristics of this person who supported me as I was going through my change process?

a. _____

b. _____

c. _____

WHAT TO EXPECT FROM A MENTOR

THINGS A MENTOR SHOULD DO:

Helps you discover & align with your goals

Listens & supports you

Asks important questions

Helps you learn

Gives specific & honest feedback related to a behaviour or action

Good Feedback:
- Focuses on what can be changed
- Offers suggestions
- Encourages self-evaluation by asking questions
- Gives feedback related to you as a person or your personality

THINGS A MENTOR SHOULD NOT DO:

Tells you what they think you need to be doing

Does your work for you

Answers all your questions

Teaches you everything

Gives feedback related to you as a person or your personality

Bad Feedback:
- Focuses on what can't be changed
- Offers instructions
- Encourages self-evaluation by making statements

WHAT A MENTOR SHOULD EXPECT FROM YOU

THINGS YOU SHOULD DO	THINGS YOU SHOULD NOT DO
Be open and willing to change and try new things	Say, "This is how I've always done it before."
Know what beliefs and assumptions you have around the process	Be unwilling to share your beliefs with your mentor
Be committed to the change and the process	Feel forced into the change and the process
Provide feedback to your mentor	Be afraid to give your mentor feedback

MENTORS TALKING ABOUT MENTORSHIP

Nobody knows the ins and outs of mentorship better than mentors. They know what it takes to guide someone down a path to bettering themselves. They have been inspired throughout their lives and have based their career on bringing about transformational change in others.

The three mentors quoted below are Paul Hurst, an executive coach and retired psychologist; Adria Trowhill, Dean of Adler

International Learning; and Renee, a well-known executive coach who wishes to remain anonymous. These three people embody what it means to be an inspired mentor. Below they share their stories of inspiration and talk about who helped them change themselves for the better throughout their lives.

Q: WHAT DOES MENTORSHIP MEAN TO YOU?

PAUL

"I think mentorship starts with an awareness, a recognition by the mentor that he or she has enough skill, experience and seasoned perspective from having been on the merry go round a number of times. It involves typically a spirit of generosity as well as a willingness to give one's time and effort, to create an opportunity for the mentee to benefit from your experience. For me, mentorship is about developing others and fulfilling oneself. Personal and professional growth and skill development is really important and has always been a part of my overarching leadership philosophy purpose. As a process, mentorship often contributes not just to the individual's development; it also helps them achieve outcomes that can be beneficial for others, including people with whom they collaborate, lead and influence."

ADRIA

"Mentorship, to me, is a relationship with somebody who is generous and selfless. My mentor had an extraordinary way of teaching. Listening to my mentor, I realized that I wasn't alone and here was somebody who had really made it, who had dealt with adversity, and so there was hope. She would say things like, 'I was more like you; I really had to work.' Her stories told me about things that had gone wrong, bad experiences she had on the stage, and that helped me a lot, so when I got discouraged I didn't feel like I didn't belong. The inspiration came from my mentor's generosity and her absolute brilliance as a teacher. And then the constant challenge. I told her about my fears, for example stage fright, and she said very matter-of-factly, 'And what else, darling? I don't care how you feel; when you get out there you're a professional and I expect you to act like a professional.' It was just a non-issue for her. She ignited a trust in myself that carried over to other areas of my life. I felt she really loved me, I felt she cared about me. I'm not saying every mentee has to be loved by their mentor, but I think there has to be some kind of a bond there for it to be really inspiring. It has to go deeper than the surface."

RENEE

"When I think of mentorship, a man by the name of Terry comes to mind. He was my swimming instructor when I was still a child. He was the toughest instructor I've ever had in my life. He wasn't mean; he was just tough. For example, he would say, 'I expect you to be here ahead of class time, early enough that you can swim around the pool ten times.' It was one of the most physically challenging classes I have ever done in my life. In another example, we had a three-metre board at the pool. I loved doing cannonballs off of the board but was afraid to dive. Terry said to me, 'Renee, unless you dive off the board, you're never going on it again.' Now here's the side of Terry that is very interesting. He then very gently coached me to dive off that board. He stayed with me as long as I stayed at the edge of the board with my arms over my head; he did not leave me. And it was very soothing and very encouraging. Now can you guess what I did next? I went right back up and dove a second time and I was never afraid to dive again because I had the experience of knowing I could do this."

Q: WHAT ARE THE CHARACTERISTICS OF A GOOD MENTOR?

PAUL

"A great deal of variety, individuality, and range of styles among mentors. Some key characteristics include a sufficient depth of experience, knowledge, professional and personal maturity. My mentor in grad school possessed all of those characteristics and was very insightful and intelligent. He helped me and many others to become more aware of self in relation to others, what our reactions were and why we were having those reactions. Through respectful dialogue he guided us through the intersections of the mind that enabled us to expand our own cognitive maps about ourselves and what was going on in our relations and interactions with clients and others. My mentor judiciously provided suggestions that we would go out and selectively try. It helped that those suggestions usually had observable positive impacts. Those results usually inspired motivation for more learning and development. Like many effective mentors he understood the importance of respectful honest feedback, directness and dialogue leading to meaning making, and creative solutions and challenges."

ADRIA

"A good mentor has to be able to connect with people at a deep level and really care about people. A mentor is a mirror for you; you can see yourself in them and vice versa. A mentor should also know that there is learning even in the worst situation. And have optimism. I think that the optimistic frame is really critical, being optimistic about them and their gifts and their capacity to learn. Having that and being non-judgemental. The continuous learning on the part of the mentor is also really critical. I don't think you can be a mentor without modelling that, along with a humility about what's still left to learn. Humility and openness go hand in hand for me. It's also important to make sure that you stay inspired as a mentor."

RENEE

"To explain, I will give you an example of my high school English teacher. Ted brought Shakespeare to life. He opened up a whole new world in the way that he taught Shakespeare. He made it interesting and exciting. One day he walked up to me and handed me a book about another culture and asked me to read it. Through this experience he offered me the idea of exploring other ways of being. The way he touched my spirit made me feel special. I went on to read other books by the same author on my own. They say a teacher appears when the student is ready. I guess he did that. He challenged me, but in a different way from Terry. He did not set out stretch goals; he just put goals in front of me. He sort of left them at my feet and said they're there for you if you want to step up to them. Another example was one my bosses early in my career. This man took me at face value for who I was and started working with me. He threw me into situations beyond my age and experience. He nurtured and guided me, but there was no stroking, and no warm fuzziness. I'm not saying he was harsh; he just showed that he trusted me and he had faith in me. More and more he would discuss things with me and seek my input. The important message from all these stories is how all these people made me feel important. And not more important than somebody else, just important in who I am, that what I'm doing is important."

Q: HOW CAN MENTORSHIP CREATE TRANS-FORMATIONAL CHANGE?

PAUL

"In those situations when transformational change is needed or wanted, mentoring can provide a safe and supportive process. Sometimes this type of impactful change occurs by mutual agreement intentionally. At other times it evolves spontaneously and unexpectedly. I've never seen it happen without some degree of unsettled emotion and dissonance in an individual's cognitive model or belief system. The moment of discovery or epiphany often is accompanied with a heightened release of emotion. It's not uncommon to experience mild shock, awe, followed by a sense of relief and accomplishment. Then the processing really starts. That was the process I experienced. I remember feeling surprised and thinking about the new learning and meaning. The mentor's patient listening, curiosity, and thoughtful comments facilitated significant changes in my perspective, enabled me to make sense of a lot of things I hadn't thought about and develop new competencies. I can't recall the specifics of the mentoring interchange, but it created life-changing and significant openings. After decades of mentoring wonderful people, my sense is that the essential pre-condition for most transformational change is the safe and trusting mentoring relationship. This relationship provides the opportunity for exploration, learning and growth to flourish."

ADRIA

"I wasn't comfortable in that neutral stance, where you don't show any emotions. It didn't feel right to me. I care for my clients passionately and it's unattached. I don't expect them to care for me passionately. I think I can tell the truth. I'm able to be tough in a way that can be heard as it's for their own good."

RENEE

"Terry put me on a pathway to becoming a competitive swimmer that I never would have expected I would go down. He put me in a position where I could see for myself that I had capacity that I didn't know I had and that I could step up to that capacity. I kept pushing and extending myself. He also opened up new doors, all new avenues of experience. One thing I've learned from my mentors is that when you're giving information to people about how they could develop as a human being, you need to do that while you're elevating them. You need to ensure the message you are delivering is that it's not that the person is bad or that they are wrong. The message needs to be that the person is fabulous and this is how they could be even better. You need to deliver that message in a way that people hear it without lowering their self-esteem. The message needs to be that this is important to pay attention to, but it doesn't make you less of a human being."

Q: WHAT IS INSPIRED MENTORSHIP?

PAUL

"Inspired mentorship is about remembering that we are dealing with the individual within the context of the organizational system. That means the mentor needs to think about what the system is about, as well as being sensitive to the individual. The inspired mentor pays attention to this interconnection of both the mentee and the organization. The inspired mentor in leadership assesses whether or not the organization has enough mentoring capacity. To be inspirational, mentors need to take into account the individual's and organization's past and present, challenging and inspiring both to achieve a better future. Inspired mentorship is also about the relationship piece; how to navigate in the mentee's world so they might think about things in a different way and expand their skill sets. I just feel a sense of satisfaction in seeing people grow and develop, seeing people being able to do what they really want and need to do, or to do what they already do even better, or to resolve something that has been a sticking point for them, or to tap into the solution that was always there but they hadn't seen it themselves. Inspirational mentors know when less is more, how to inspire through example, initiate conversations that enable individuals to find their own solutions, know when to push and give direction, and respect the mentee's right to learn from mistakes."

ADRIA

"The people that stand out are the people who actually become their future self in the mentoring process. For me, it meets me at my intellectual level, wherever that is. I need to know that I'm understood, seen and heard. And being acknowledged, that goes along with seeing who I am. People who see a person they're mentoring really see, and see more than the actual mentee sees: see strengths that are not integrated, for example. Also, I think there's reciprocity in learning."

RENEE

"My next mentor is someone I would not normally refer to as a mentor, but I had the opportunity to observe him in action many times. The first time I met him there was something very major happening in the corporation that he was involved in, but did not know about until later. And yet, when I walked into his office, he sat down, leaned back, and said, 'Ok, what are we here to talk about?' He acted as if there was nothing else more important than that meeting. Later that day I found out he had had an important meeting with the board of directors. A few years later I had the opportunity to give him some feedback. I said, 'The way you treat people, you make them feel as though they are the most important thing in your life at that moment.' This man had incredible integrity. He did what he said he was going to do, and if he wasn't going to do something, he'd let you know and he'd let you know why. He was just an incredible leader to observe."

FIVE QUESTIONS FOR REFLECTION:
INSPIRED MENTORSHIP

1. WHO WOULD YOU CONSIDER TO BE AN INSPIRED MENTOR AND WHY?

_____

_____

_____

_____

2. WHAT IS THE MOST PROFOUND LEARNING YOU WALKED AWAY WITH FROM YOUR RELATIONSHIP WITH YOUR MENTOR?

_____

_____

_____

_____

3. IF YOU WERE TO HIRE A MENTOR, WHAT WOULD BE THE MOST IMPORTANT CHARACTERISTIC THEY WOULD NEED TO HAVE IN ORDER TO SUCCESSFULLY WORK WITH YOU?

_____

_____

_____

_____

4. WHEN YOU ARE STUCK OR CANNOT MOVE FORWARD, HOW CAN A MENTOR MOST HELP YOU?

_____

_____

_____

_____

5. IF YOU WERE YOUR OWN MENTOR, WHAT WOULD YOU TELL YOURSELF IS MOST IMPORTANT TO THE SUCCESS OF THE CHANGE YOU ARE CURRENTLY GOING THROUGH?

_____

_____

_____

_____

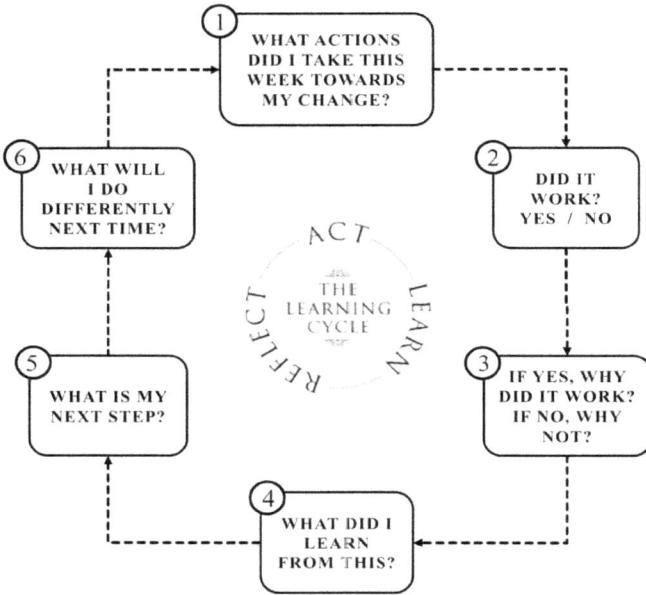

1. _____

2. _____

3. _____

4. _____

5. _____

6. _____

Trusting your Process

"As soon as you trust yourself, you will know how to live."
- Johann Wolfgang von Goethe

How Do I Trust My Way of Making Change?

As you work through your process of change, it is worth reflecting on how you have made this change happen in your life. Force yourself to pay attention to each one of your steps. Do not drift or tune out' of yourself, but stop and notice when you have had a success or a failure.

Take Time to Reflect

Questions to ask yourself:

In the most recent success that I have experienced, what was my initial goal?

_____

_____

What actually happened?

_____

_____

Looking back on this success, what did I learn about my process that led to success?

_____

_____

What surprises did I have along the way? How did I adjust to ensure my success?

_____

_____

What did I learn about who I needed to be throughout my process? (e.g. focused, courageous, open, honest, authentic, etc.)

_____

_____

HONOUR THE WAY YOU DREAM

Be mindful every day that your process is unique to you. Trusting your process is about remembering your strengths that will help you move through the natural obstacles and difficulties that always arise when going through change. Know yourself and give yourself the things that most serve you.

ENERGY: Tap into your energy.

What keeps me going and brings me into the best possible place for me to achieve my goal?

_____

_____

What gives me balance and calm during times of change?

_____

_____

FOCUS: Dreams can create confusion and clutter from all of your different ideas, options, and pathways.

What do I need to do to stay focused on my goal?

_____

_____

What most often distracts me and takes me away from following my goal?

_____

_____

Find an easy way to reduce your clutter and stay focused on your final goal, because when you follow your dreams, you can lose sight of them easily in the midst of confusion and, sometimes, disappointment.

SUPPORT: There may come a time when you have to admit to yourself that you cannot do this alone. Look at the relationships that have supported you and made a difference in your life or partnerships that encourage you tc be your best, strongest, healthiest person.

Who can most help me to stay on track towards achieving my goal?

_____

_____

In what ways do these people most help me to get to where I want to go?

_____

_____

Bring those people towards you and nurture those people. Every relationship is a give and take. Add value where you can and ask for what you need.

Setting goals and achieving them are a vital part of success. Author and Motivational Speaker Raymond Aaron has written a bestselling book *Double Your Income Doing What You Love.* For a free download of Mr. Aaron's book, go to his website, www.aaron.com.

RECOGNIZING THE DIFFERENCE BETWEEN THE INNER CRITIC AND THE INNER FRIEND

As you are moving through your process, be in full awareness of the emergence of your Inner Critic. Learn how to recognize the way this voice can influence your decisions. Accept the Inner Critic as part of your process because it is natural. It will often judge not only what you are doing, but you as a person. It can still be possible, and sometimes necessary, to honour the gifts that the Inner Critic can bring you when it warns you against certain things. However, do not allow it to take over and stop you from achieving your goal or making the change that you want.

One way to balance between the negatives and positives that the Inner Critic can bring is by recognizing its voice versus your own true voice, or the voice of your Inner Friend. Make a distinction between these two, and when all you can hear is the Inner Critic, ask your Inner Friend to show up.

THE VOICE OF THE INNER CRITIC:

Your Inner Critic wants you to protect what you know, what you are sure of, and what is in your comfort zone.

The Inner Critic asks, "What's wrong?" "What could go wrong?" "Am I safe?" "Am I still in my comfort zone?" "Are you sure this is the right thing?" "Who are you to do this anyways?" "Why not wait until you're really sure?" "What's really going to be different this time?"

The Inner Critic can also bring you gifts. It can protect you, ensure you are safe and minimize risk. Lower the volume of the Inner Critic and ask it, "Of all this, what do you most want me to pay attention to?" Listen to its suggestion and consider it, but do not allow it to stop you from moving forward.

THE VOICE OF THE INNER FRIEND:

Your Inner Friend works from a place of what can be, of possibility.

The Inner Friend asks, "So what is the best you have to work with?" "What can be possible?" "What support can you get?" "What are you learning from this process?" "What will this give you in the future?"

In times of change, find your Inner Friend. As Marilee Adams says in her book *Change Your Questions, Change Your Life,* be aware of your Inner Critic, know it, know its voice and its sayings, then choose another way of thinking and move forward. Once you are aware of these voices, you can more accurately make the choice that is right for you.

FIVE QUESTIONS FOR REFLECTION:
TRUSTING YOUR PROCESS

1. HOW HAS YOUR INNER CRITIC STOPPED YOU FROM ACHIEVING YOUR DREAMS?

_____

_____

_____

_____

2. HOW HAS YOUR INNER FRIEND HELPED YOU TO REALIZE YOUR DREAMS?

_____

_____

_____

_____

3. WHAT ARE THE FAVOURITE SAYINGS OF YOUR INNER FRIEND?

_____

_____

_____

_____

4. GIVEN THE CHANGE YOU MAKE TO MAKE, WHAT SAYINGS WILL MOST HELP YOU TO ACHIEVE YOUR GOAL?

_____

_____

_____

_____

5. WHAT DO YOU MOST TRUST ABOUT YOUR PROCESS OF CHANGE AND HOW HAS IT HELPED YOU MAKE THIS CHANGE SUCCESSFUL?

_____

_____

_____

_____

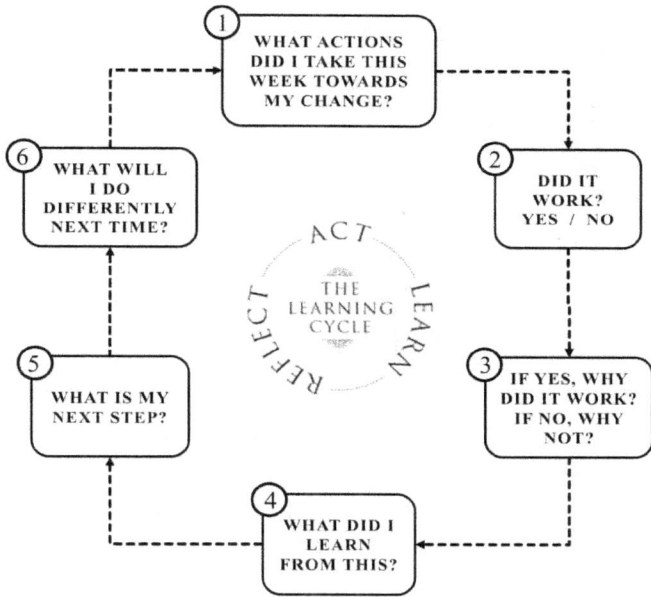

1. _____

2. _____

3. _____

4. _____

5. _____

6. _____

7 Stories of Getting Unstuck

"It always seems impossible until it's done."
- Nelson Mandela

Change is an Inside-Out Process

Nancy had been working a corporate job for the past 6 years; she had four kids and a loving husband, but something was not aligned for Nancy and she was not completely happy. One day, she looked in the mirror and asked herself, "What do I really want?" The answer that came to her was an unusual one for someone her age. The answer was dancing. Nancy immersed herself completely in this new hobby. It took a lot of courage to be vulnerable on stage and in front of the other younger, more experienced dancers. But Nancy had finally found a way to express her creativity. She learned to trust herself and it gave her confidence to know that she was able to learn something she never thought she could. Nancy went through a transformational change; she was doing what she loved, expressing herself, and becoming less stressed about work. Nancy's entire family benefited from her change, she was happier. She eventually left her corporate job and started her own business. Nancy's change happened with the inside first. Discovering what inspired her and trusting her inner heart gave her the confidence to do what she truly loved and be happier in her life choices.

COACHING OR MENTORSHIP CAN SHOW YOU THE PROPER WAY OF MAKING CHANGE

As a motivational speaker, Donna travelled a lot. It was a lonely lifestyle and she craved companionship constantly. Donna had a successful career, but she was not happy in her personal life. She was out of shape and lonely. She had a coach who knew that she had a strong need for routine and suggested she look into fostering a puppy for Dog Guides of Canada, an organization focused on training guide dogs. Her coach believed that not only would being a foster mom be good for Donna physically, it would also be good for her emotionally. She was right. As Donna focused on training the puppy, she became more physically fit and was spending more time away from the office. She was less stressed, more relaxed, and loved building a routine around the puppy's needs. She brought the puppy with her when she travelled and her coach and her family could see the change in her lifestyle and attitude almost immediately. Donna was delighted to have a companion who needed her and her love. She learned that being responsible for someone other than herself was rewarding. Knowing that by helping others she was actually helping herself changed the way she lived her life. Today, Donna mentors young people and new immigrants, helping them as they work to accomplish their goals in a new country.

ONE SMALL CHANGE CAN MAKE ALL THE DIFFERENCE

Mark started out as a sprinter. Hurdles are not something that is natural for any athlete. Mark started hurdling because he was not fast enough to be a sprinter and he wanted to fulfill his dream of competing in the Olympics. In 1980, at the age of 18, he qualified to represent Canada at the Olympic Games in Moscow (his first of 5 Olympic teams). Within the next six years, he won two Gold medals at the Commonwealth Games, in the 110m hurdles and another in the 4 x 100 relay. Mark was extremely passionate about what he did. He loved competing and knew with hard work, he could compete with the best in the world. Most of his time was spent training and, just like any other amateur athlete, Mark's dream was to win the Olympic Gold for his country. However, no matter how hard he trained or how many games he competed in, Mark was not reaching his full potential as an athlete. He went through a frustrating streak of placing fourth place and knocking down hurdles in almost every final he raced in. Knowing he had to make some sort of a change if he hoped to win a gold medal, Mark went to work under the tutelage of the world's best coaches. This coach suggested that one of Mark's feet was slightly turned out by 1" and that realigning his foot would make a huge difference. Mark had an open mind and knew that he had room to improve, so he realigned his foot by 1" and the difference he noticed was truly life-changing. In the 1992 Olympic Games in Barcelona, Mark McKoy won the Gold Medal for Canada in the 110m hurdles by 39"! (the exact amount of crooked steps Mark usually took in a race). This was the first Gold medal for Canadian track and field in 60 years.

CHANGE IS AN ACTION WORD, SO TAKE ACTION NOW TO BEGIN THE CHANGE YOU WANT TO MAKE

Michele was an out of work 20-something year old who had been trying to break into the movie industry for years with no luck. She sent in resume after resume but never heard anything back and felt stuck working for her father just to make ends meet. One day she said to herself, "I have to make my own success." She thought about what she was good at, what skills she had, and how she could turn that into a business. She immediately thought of babysitting; she had been taking care of children for years and she knew she had the wisdom and experience to turn this into something lucrative. She started her own Nanny Placement Agency. One photo shoot with her friend's baby later she had created a logo, business cards, and a basic website. Within a month of taking action, Michele had five clients who were paying her significant placement fees to find nannies for their children. Michele did not wait for something to happen to her; she made change happen by taking action.

THE HARDEST STEP IS THE FIRST CHANGE

It took Wendy 8 years to leave a bad relationship. She was at the theatre, coincidentally sitting beside her ex-husband and his new wife, when it finally hit her: "My life sucks." Wendy realized that the same was not working anymore and she needed to make a change. The best way for her to do this was to completely remove herself from the familiar and experience something different, so she rented out her house and moved to rural France for six months. When she came home, she began to make courageous business choices. She used her creative skills and made unique business moves, doing things she had never done before. Wendy had reminded herself of who she was and the kind of difference she wanted to make. She had found the courage to step out and do completely new and different things and she was no longer settling for second best. As a result of Wendy's creativity being unleashed, she published a book and brought her business to a new level.

Making a change, trying new and different things, and making decisions that were right for her, all meant that Wendy was finally getting to live the life she wanted to live.

CHANGE BEGINS, CONTINUES, AND ENDS WITH GOALS, THE RIGHT MINDSET AND THE RIGHT ATTITUDE

At 27 years old, Daniel lived at home with his parents and was working as a bouncer at a bar. He was content, Daniel was always content, but he had no direction or plan for the future. He knew he could not live like this forever, but he had no desire to make a big change. Until one fell into his lap. His older brother approached him with a business idea. He wanted to open a contracting company but he needed Daniel to run it. Daniel had never done anything like this before and the idea of running a business was daunting. He struggled with the idea of taking on so much responsibility, but eventually realized this was something he needed to do. He needed to challenge himself. Daniel and his brother came up with a business plan and Daniel knew he was capable of running a successful business. Once he had the right mindset, Daniel felt only excitement at the idea. He had always wanted to work with his hands and this felt like the right decision for him. Two years later, Daniel was doing so well that he was able to buy his brother out and become the sole owner of his business.

CHANGE REQUIRES YOU TO STEP OUT OF YOUR COMFORT ZONE AND DO THINGS YOU HAVE NEVER DONE BEFORE

Tom had never really known what he wanted to "be" when he grew up. He went through high school and University doing only what was required of him; going to classes and getting good grades but spending the rest of his time socializing with friends. After graduating, he ended up in a typical office job where he sat at his desk, did his work, and went home at 5:00pm sharp. After two years at his job, Tom realized he was unhappy. He wanted to quit but he did not know what he could do that would make him happy, so he stayed where he was. Six months later, Tom's work environment had become toxic. He did not truly care about his job, he did not respect his bosses or his colleagues, and he let it show. He had let it get to the point where he had no choice but to leave. Because of his inability to act, Tom ended up unemployed with no idea of what he wanted to do with his life. But instead of feeling sorry for himself, Tom started to do things he had never done before. He volunteered, he contributed to his community, he joined groups and met new people. He started to figure out what his interests were and doing things because he wanted to, not because he had to. Tom learned what he liked, what he was good at, and gained experience. He eventually found his dream job at a publishing company and is happy and motivated at work.

ACT
THE
LEARNING
CYCLE
REFLECT
LEARN

DID YOU ACCOMPLISH YOUR GOAL?

YES   NO

"It had long since come to my attention that people of accomplishment rarely sat back and let things happen to them. They went out and happened to things."

- Leonardo Da Vinci

ACKNOWLEDGEMENTS

I deeply appreciate the wisdom of my business coach, Sherry Lowry. A great deal of insight in this book originated in coaching sessions with my coach and the experience I had going through my own change journey.

I am blessed with and grateful for the consistency and clarity that came from my editor, Liz Culotti, whose tireless support and commitment allowed this book to be born. I gave her many tasks and lots of materials which she simplified brilliantly to help me create this book.

I am indebted to the Raymond Aaron Group for their dedication and support in producing this book. Their team of supportive and highly skilled professionals showed me the way to finally publishing the book that has been inside of me for so many years.

A big thank you to my colleagues Paul Hurst and Adria Trowhill. I am grateful for the support and for their willingness to share their time and wisdom within this book. Also thank you to Mark McKoy and Donna Messer for sharing their stories of change and for their insight and support.

I want to humbly acknowledge all my clients around the world who have been loyal to me, who have learned from me and from whom I have also learned so much.

A special thank you to my colleague and friend, Darlene Chrissley, for inspiring and unleashing the creative spirit within me.

I am grateful to my family who are my rock and foundation; my daughters, Erin and Samantha, and my sons, Sean and David. They have taught me about change throughout the years and I am blessed to have them in my life.

Of course I do not have the words to express the forever strong and consistent strength of my husband Mike, whose eternal support I have at home. There is nothing more that I could ever ask for and I am so grateful.

I dedicate this book to my husband Mike.

ABOUT THE AUTHOR

Lydia Roy is an author, international executive coach, business consultant, and facilitator with over 20 years of experience.

In 2001, Lydia started her own company, Star Coaching International, based in Toronto, Canada. Specializing in leadership, Lydia has supported thousands of clients to successfully grow their businesses and change their lives.

Lydia has cross-industry experience and has worked with CEOs and Executives in a broad range of industries, including major financial institutions and health care organizations.

Lydia is also a Mentor to other coaches and has delivered programs around the world leading to the certification of hundreds of new coaches.

Lydia currently lives in Toronto, Ontario, with her husband, dog Jake, and four children.

For more information on Lydia, please visit: www.lydiaroy.com.

STARCOACHING
INTERNATIONAL

www.ingramcontent.com/pod-product-compliance
Lightning Source LLC
Chambersburg PA
CBHW071114210326
41519CB00020B/6290

* 9 7 8 1 9 2 7 6 7 7 8 5 8 *